LIVING WITH THE DINOSAURS

HORSESHOE CRABS
LIVED WITH THE DINOSAURS!

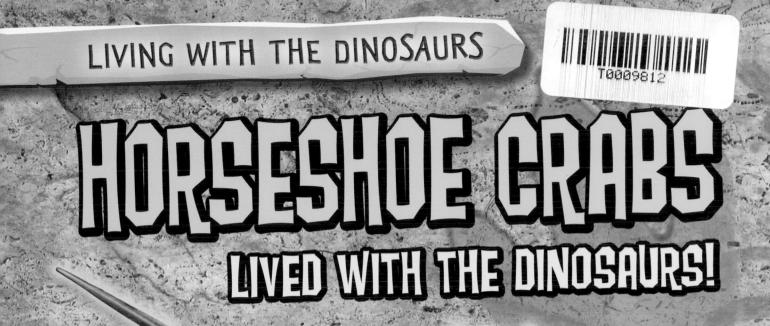

BY SARAH MACHAJEWSKI

Gareth Stevens
PUBLISHING

Please visit our website, www.garethstevens.com. For a free color catalog of all our high-quality books, call toll free 1-800-542-2595 or fax 1-877-542-2596.

Cataloging-in-Publication Data

Names: Machajewski, Sarah.
Title: Horseshoe crabs lived with the dinosaurs! / Sarah Machajewski.
Description: New York : Gareth Stevens Publishing, 2017. | Series: Living with the dinosaurs | Includes index.
Identifiers: ISBN 9781482456530 (pbk.) | ISBN 9781482456561 (library bound) | ISBN 9781482456547 (6 pack)
Subjects: LCSH: Merostomata–Juvenile literature.
Classification: LCC QL447.7 M33 2017 | DDC 595.4'92–dc23

First Edition

Published in 2017 by
Gareth Stevens Publishing
111 East 14th Street, Suite 349
New York, NY 10003

Designer: Laura Bowen
Editor: Therese Shea

Photo credits: Cover, p. 1 (horseshoe crab) ShaneKato/E+/Getty Images; cover, p. 1 (footprints) nemlaza/Shutterstock.com; cover, pp. 1–24 (background) Natalia Davidovich/Shutterstock.com; cover, pp. 1–24 (stone boxes) Daria Yakovleva/Shutterstock.com; p. 5 (horseshoe crab) Ilya D. Gridnev/Shutterstock.com; p. 5 (inset) Linda Bucklin/Shutterstock.com; p. 6 Catmando/Shutterstock.com; p. 7 Wild Horizon/Universal Images Group/Getty Images; p. 9 Ethan Daniels/Shutterstock.com; p. 11 (both) Butterfly Hunter/Shutterstock.com; p. 12 Fresnel/Shutterstock.com; pp. 13, 17 Robert F. Sisson/National Geographic/Getty Images; p. 14 Cropbot/Wikimedia Commons; p. 15 The Washington Post/Getty Images; p. 16 Christos Georghiou/Shutterstock.com; p. 18 Smallbones/Wikimedia Commons; p. 19 Elliotte Rusty Harold/Shutterstock.com; p. 20 blewisphotography/Shutterstock.com; p. 21 Rodger Jackman/Oxford Scientific.

Printed in China

CPSIA compliance information: Batch #CW17GS: For further information contact Gareth Stevens, New York, New York at 1-800-542-2595.

CONTENTS

Words in the glossary appear in **bold** type the first time they are used in the text.

FROM ANOTHER TIME

What was Earth like when dinosaurs **roamed** the planet? Scientists think dinosaurs first lived about 245 million years ago. Humans weren't alive then, so we don't have any records of it. Some species, or kinds, of animals that were around back then are still here today. Horseshoe crabs are one of them. They're almost 450 million years old!

Horseshoe crabs are ancient creatures. They even look like something out of another time. How has this species survived all these years? Let's take a closer look and find out.

THE PREHISTORIC WORLD

Plateosaurus was a dinosaur that walked on all fours and was nearly 30 feet (9 m) long. Horseshoe crabs didn't have to worry, though. Plateosaurus was a plant eater.

Plateosaurus

A HORSESHOE CRAB CAN LIVE TO BE 20 YEARS OLD. HOWEVER, THE HORSESHOE CRAB SPECIES IS PREHISTORIC. THAT MEANS IT WAS AROUND BEFORE RECORDED HISTORY!

5

VERY, VERY OLD

Horseshoe crabs have been on Earth longer than most creatures alive today. They lived before people, dinosaurs, and flying bugs. **Fossils** of the horseshoe crab's **ancestors** have been found that are between 444 million and 488 million years old!

Today's horseshoe crabs look a lot like the horseshoe crabs that date back to about 200 million years ago. They haven't changed much since then. For that reason, horseshoe crabs are sometimes called "living fossils."

pterosaur

THE PREHISTORIC WORLD

Horseshoe crabs once shared their world with the flying pterosaur, which was a cousin of the dinosaurs. One species was 33 feet (10 m) from the tip of one wing to the other!

THIS HORSESHOE CRAB FOSSIL IS BETWEEN 145 MILLION AND 161 MILLION YEARS OLD. THE REMAINS LOOK LIKE A HORSESHOE CRAB YOU'D SEE TODAY.

AMAZING ARTHROPODS

Horseshoe crabs belong to a group of animals called arthropods. Bugs, spiders, and true crabs are arthropods, too. Though their name may suggest something else, horseshoe crabs aren't true crabs at all. They belong to their own class of animals called Merostomata (mehr-uh-STOH-muh-duh).

There are four species of horseshoe crabs. They live in different areas of the world. One kind lives along the eastern coast of North America and in the Gulf of Mexico. The other three species live in the waters of Asia, from Japan to India.

THE FOUR SPECIES OF HORSESHOE CRABS LOOK SIMILAR. THE SPECIES IN NORTH AMERICA, *LIMULUS POLYPHEMUS*, IS ALSO CALLED THE AMERICAN HORSESHOE CRAB OR ATLANTIC HORSESHOE CRAB.

Horseshoe Crab Range

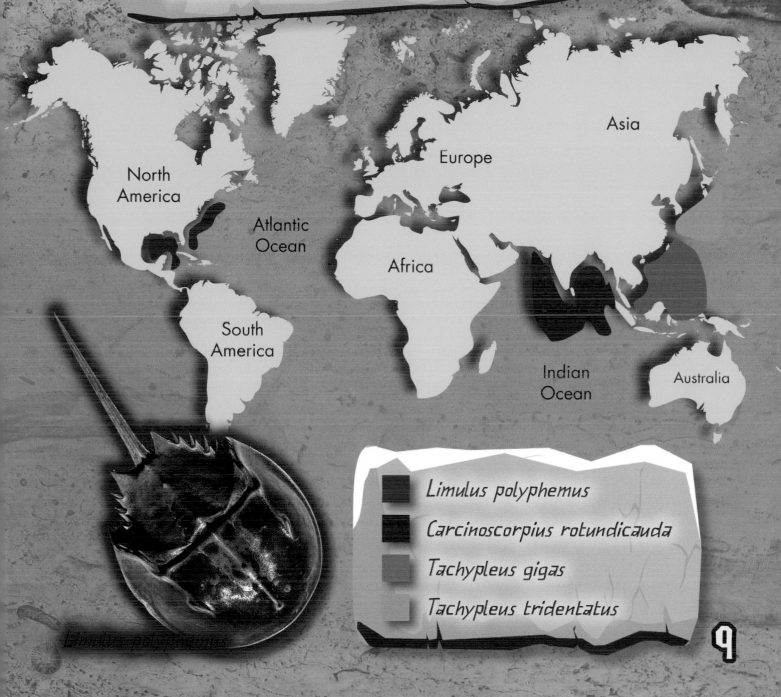

- Asia
- Europe
- North America
- Atlantic Ocean
- Africa
- South America
- Indian Ocean
- Australia

Limulus polyphemus

Legend:
- Limulus polyphemus
- Carcinoscorpius rotundicauda
- Tachypleus gigas
- Tachypleus tridentatus

9

ANCIENT BODY

The horseshoe crab hasn't changed much over millions of years. Its body is divided into three parts. The head, or prosoma, holds the brain, heart, and mouth. It has six pairs of legs. The first pair is used for catching prey. The other five pairs help the horseshoe crab walk and eat.

The abdomen contains **muscles** for movement and **gills** for breathing. The tail, or telson, is the third main body part. If a horseshoe crab ends up on its back, it uses its telson to flip over.

EVERY PART OF THE HORSESHOE CRAB'S BODY HAS HELPED THE SPECIES SURVIVE OVER MILLIONS OF YEARS. A HARD SHELL PROTECTS THE HEAD AND ALL ITS IMPORTANT PARTS. SPINES PROTECT THE ABDOMEN. THE LONG, POINTED TAIL HELPS IT STAY RIGHT SIDE UP.

Horseshoe Crab Anatomy

TOP (HARD SHELL)

TELSON

HEAD

UNDERSIDE

ABDOMEN

GILLS

MOUTH

LEGS

SEEING IN WATER

Horseshoe crabs live in deep oceans and near coastal beaches. Their bodies have **adapted** to their watery **habitats**. They have many eyes that help them find their way.

Two **compound eyes** are on each side of the shell. They're used for finding **mates**. Five eyes on top of the shell sense sunlight and a special kind of light people can't see, called ultraviolet light. Two eyes on the underside of its body near its mouth help the horseshoe crab know where it is when it's swimming.

Spinosaurus

THE PREHISTORIC WORLD

The dinosaur *Spinosaurus* swam in ancient waters, just like the horseshoe crab. It's the only known swimming dinosaur. *Spinosaurus* had a large fin-like part on its back and paddle-like feet.

HORSESHOE CRABS' EYES HAVEN'T CHANGED MUCH OVER MILLIONS OF YEARS. STUDIES OF THEIR EYES HAVE TAUGHT US A LOT ABOUT OUR OWN EYES.

SPAWN POINT

The horseshoe crab's survival depends on an activity as ancient as the crab itself. In early summer, horseshoe crabs leave the ocean at night and arrive on beaches for their **spawning** season. Horseshoe crabs sense the moon's ultraviolet light and know when it's time to spawn.

Female horseshoe crabs swim to beaches to lay their eggs. Nearby males locate them, and mates arrive on the beach together. The female lays hundreds of eggs in nests.

Hadrosaurus foulkii

THE PREHISTORIC WORLD

Fossils of the duck-billed dinosaur, *Hadrosaurus foulkii*, have been found in the Delaware Bay area of the United States, the same place where many horseshoe crabs spawn.

THE DELAWARE BAY IS THE LARGEST SPAWNING POINT IN THE WORLD FOR HORSESHOE CRABS. THE ACTIVITY YOU SEE IN THIS PICTURE HAS BEEN HAPPENING FOR MILLIONS OF YEARS—LONG BEFORE PEOPLE WERE AROUND TO PHOTOGRAPH IT.

THE LIFE CYCLE

Horseshoe crab eggs hatch, or break open, after about 2 weeks. Larvae come out. The larvae look like tiny horseshoe crab adults with smaller tails.

After hatching, larvae leave their nest and head into the water. They settle into the sandy ocean floor. There, they undergo their first molt, which is when they lose their shell to make room for more growth. Juvenile, or young, horseshoe crabs molt many times before they become adults. As horseshoe crabs grow, they move into deeper water.

Diplodocus

THE PREHISTORIC WORLD

Horseshoe crabs grow to be as long as 19 inches (48 cm), though males are a bit smaller. That's small compared to some dinosaurs! The *Diplodocus* was 85 feet (26 m) long!

HORSESHOE CRABS ARE GREAT SURVIVORS. UNLESS THEY'RE FEEDING, JUVENILE HORSESHOE CRABS SPEND THEIR TIME BURIED IN THE SANDY OCEAN FLOOR. THERE THEY HIDE FROM BIRDS, SEA TURTLES, AND TRUE CRABS THAT LIKE TO EAT THEM.

horseshoe crab eggs

AN IMPORTANT ROLE

An ecosystem is a community of creatures that depend on each other for survival. As part of an ecosystem for nearly 450 million years, the horseshoe crab plays a very important role for other animals.

Countless animal species have come to depend on it as a food source. Fish, true crabs, sea snails, shorebirds, and sea turtles feed on eggs and larvae. Some animals—such as sponges, snails, mud crabs, and sand shrimp—actually live on and inside the horseshoe crab's shell!

snails living on horseshoe crab shell

THE RED KNOT IS A SHOREBIRD THAT DEPENDS ON HORSESHOE CRAB EGGS TO FUEL ITS LONG FLIGHT NORTH. IF HORSESHOE CRAB POPULATIONS SUFFER, RED KNOT POPULATIONS SUFFER, TOO.

MILLIONS OF YEARS FROM NOW

Horseshoe crabs lived for a very long time without humans. However, now that we share Earth, we must keep it a good home for all creatures. We must keep our waters clean so horseshoe crabs have a healthy habitat. We can also make sure beaches are clear so they can spawn there.

Horseshoe crabs have already survived millions of years of change. They once lived with dinosaurs. Now they live with us. Who will these ancient creatures live with in the future?

EARTH WAS VERY DIFFERENT WHEN HORSESHOE CRABS FIRST APPEARED. HOW DIFFERENT WILL IT LOOK 450 MILLION YEARS FROM NOW?

Horseshoe Crabs: Adapted for Survival

telson to keep upright

hard shell to protect its body

blood can fight tiny creatures called bacteria that are harmful

many eyes to sense different kinds of light

gills help it breathe in and out of water

many legs for eating, walking, digging, catching prey

GLOSSARY

adapt: to change to suit conditions

ancestor: someone who comes before others in their family tree

compound eye: an eye that's made of many parts

fossil: the hardened marks or remains of plants and animals that formed over thousands or millions of years

gill: the body part that ocean animals use to breathe in water

habitat: the natural place where an animal or plant lives

mate: one of a pair of animals that comes together to make babies

muscle: the part of the body that produces movement

protect: to keep safe

roam: to walk far and wide

spawning: laying eggs in large numbers

spine: a long, sharp body part

FOR MORE INFORMATION

BOOKS

Hemstock, Annie Wendt. *Horseshoe Crabs.* New York, NY: PowerKids Press, 2015.

Schnell, Lisa Kahn. *High Tide for Horseshoe Crabs.* Watertown, MA: Charlesbridge, 2015.

WEBSITES

The Amazing Horseshoe
horseshoecrab.org/nh/hist.html
Learn all about horseshoe crabs with this cool resource.

Dinosaurs Quiz
discoverykids.com/games/dinosaurs-quiz/
Do you know a lot about dinosaurs? Take this quiz!

Welcome to Kids Dinos
www.kidsdinos.com
Explore the world of dinosaurs on this fun site.

INDEX